HORSING AROUND

CLYDESDALES

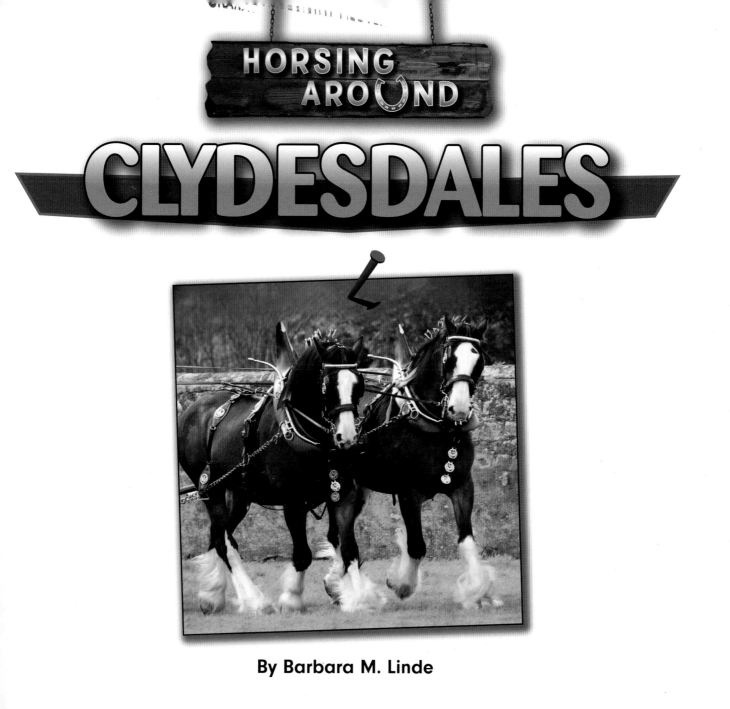

By Barbara M. Linde

Gareth Stevens
Publishing

Please visit our website, www.garethstevens.com. For a free color catalog of all our high-quality books, call toll free 1-800-542-2595 or fax 1-877-542-2596.

A special thanks to Patricia Howell of Merry Mount Farms in Toano, Virginia, and Suzanne Thiele-Thornton of Felicity Arabians in Carrollton, Virginia, for their time and knowledge.

Library of Congress Cataloging-in-Publication Data

Linde, Barbara M.
Clydesdales / Barbara M. Linde.
    p. cm. — (Horsing around)
Includes index.
ISBN 978-1-4339-6466-4 (pbk.)
ISBN 978-1-4339-6467-1 (6-pack)
ISBN 978-1-4339-6464-0 (library binding)
1. Clydesdale horse—Juvenile literature. I. Title.
SF293.C65L56 2012
636.15—dc23
                                            2011026019

First Edition

Published in 2012 by
Gareth Stevens Publishing
111 East 14th Street, Suite 349
New York, NY 10003

Copyright © 2012 Gareth Stevens Publishing

Designer: Michael J. Flynn
Editor: Therese Shea

Photo credits: Cover, p. 1 iStockphoto.com; (cover, back cover, p. 1 wooden sign), (front cover, back cover, pp. 2–4, 7–8, 11–12, 15–16, 19–24 wood background), 5, 6, 7, 10, 16–17, 18, 20 Shutterstock.com; p. 9 Radius Images/Getty Images; p. 13 Keystone-France/Gamma-Keystone/Getty Images; p. 14 Tim Graham Photo Library/Tim Graham Royal Photos/Getty Images.

Printed in the United States of America

CPSIA compliance information: Batch #CW12GS: For further information contact Gareth Stevens, New York, New York at 1-800-542-2595.

Contents

Words in the glossary appear in **bold** type the first time they are used in the text.

What Is a Clydesdale?

Have you seen a tall, heavy horse pulling a big load? It was probably a Clydesdale! A Clydesdale is usually between 16 and 18 **hands** high at its shoulders, or withers. This is between 64 and 72 inches (163 and 183 cm) tall. It's one of the largest of all horse **breeds**.

Clydesdales are powerful, handsome, and intelligent. In recent years, these horses have become easy to recognize for their size and shape. This breed is also respected for working hard.

THE MANE FACT

Clydesdales usually weigh between 1,600 and 1,800 pounds (726 and 817 kg). Some weigh as much as 2,200 pounds (999 kg)!

A full-grown
Clydesdale
weighs as much
as a small car!

Many people who raise Clydesdales want them to have a solid coat color with white markings on their face and legs.

THE MANE FACT

A Clydesdale's feather helps drain water away from its heels and hoofs, keeping them dry and healthy.

Clydesdales are known for the long white hair on their lower legs. This soft hair is called feather.

A Clydesdale has a flat face and a wide **muzzle**. Many have a white mark on their face called a blaze. They hold their head high in the air. Their back is short, and their legs are thick. This makes them look powerful.

The most common Clydesdale coat color is reddish-brown, or bay. Other Clydesdale colors are black, brown, and chestnut.

feather

7

A Special Walk

A Clydesdale's way of walking, or gait, is different from most horses' gait. As it walks, a Clydesdale lifts each hoof high off the ground. If you stand behind the horse, you can see the bottom of each hoof as it goes up. The horse is heavy, but it looks graceful and proud as it walks.

Clydesdales have bigger feet than most horses. They're often more than 20 inches (51 cm) long! Clydesdales usually wear horseshoes that weigh about 5 pounds (2 kg) each.

THE MANE FACT

A Clydesdale's foot is about twice the size of a Thoroughbred's foot. Each foot is as big as a dinner plate!

Like shoes for people, horseshoes are made to keep horses' feet safe and healthy.

Clydesdales are still the most common **draft** horses in Scotland.

THE MANE FACT

The name "Clydesdale" was first used for this horse breed in 1826.

Early Clydesdales

The Clydesdale breed started in Lanarkshire, Scotland, in the 1700s. This area was once called Clydesdale because it's on the River Clyde. Scottish workers needed strong draft horses for their farms and businesses. Some breeders brought two strong **stallions** from northwestern Europe. These horses were bred with local **mares**.

By the early 1800s, people all over Scotland and England used these strong horses. Beginning in the late 1800s, Scottish settlers took the horses to Canada, the United States, Australia, and New Zealand.

Over the years, Clydesdales have been used for many purposes. Long ago, knights rode heavy draft horses into battle. These were the **ancestors** of Clydesdales.

Hundreds of years later, Scottish people used their Clydesdales for hard work. Clydesdales have the strength needed to pull farmers' plows. They can pull thousands of pounds. Their big, heavy feet are perfect for walking though muddy farm fields. In cities, these horses pulled carts filled with goods as well as wagons carrying people.

THE MANE FACT

The Clydesdale Horse Society began in Scotland in 1877. The Clydesdale Breeders of the U.S.A. started in 1879.

When the buses weren't running in Scotland, people turned to Clydesdales to get them around!

13

This Clydesdale, carrying a drummer and his drums, marches in a birthday parade for the queen of England.

THE MANE FACT

There are about 5,000 Clydesdales around the world. The United States has more Clydesdales than any other country.

Modern Work

Because of their beauty and strength, Clydesdales are fun to watch. In cities, they pull **carriages** of people through parks. Many farmers and loggers around the world still use Clydesdales. These powerful horses can go where machines can't, such as through forests.

In England, members of the Queen's Household **Cavalry** ride Clydesdales. A few of these horses carry very heavy parade drums in addition to a rider.

Some people make money raising and selling Clydesdales. Others use Clydesdales to sell goods. You may have seen Clydesdales on TV **commercials**.

15

A hitch is a group of Clydesdales connected together to pull a heavy load. Each horse in a hitch has a **harness**. The harnesses are joined together. A driver uses reins to give directions.

In a hitch pulling a plow, the horses closest to the plow are called wheelhorses. They're the strongest because they have to pull, slow, and stop the plow. The swing horses in the middle turn the plow. The leaders in the front of the hitch are the fastest horses.

Drivers and horses in a hitch practice many hours working as a team.

17

Clydesdales easily pull wagons full of people. People like watching the Clydesdales as much as their surroundings!

THE MANE FACT

The number of Clydesdales was very low in the 1970s. Today, however, the breed is no longer in danger of dying out.

Clydesdales for Fun

Often called "gentle giants," Clydesdales are great around children. They're perfect for trail riding. People ride them in shows, too. Surprisingly, these big, heavy horses can be good jumpers. Some owners offer the use of their Clydesdales to help **disabled** or sick people. Clydesdale hitches are entered in contests to pull heavy loads. Clydesdales are favorites in parades as well.

The Clydesdale Breeders of the U.S.A. helps people learn about Clydesdales. It also puts on events for members to show off their beautiful horses.

Clydesdales need healthy food and fresh water. Adults eat from 25 to 50 pounds (11 to 23 kg) of hay each day. They may eat 2 to 10 pounds (1 to 5 kg) of grain or other feed, too.

Clydesdales should see an animal doctor, or veterinarian, for regular checkups and teeth cleaning. They can get a skin condition called mud fever around their feet. Cleaning and clipping their feather may help prevent this. Daily brushing is also good for Clydesdales' coats.

Clydesdales need exercise to keep healthy.

The Clydesdale Timeline

1700s	The first Clydesdales are bred in Scotland.
1800s	Scottish settlers take Clydesdales to Canada, the United States, and other countries.
1826	"Clydesdale" is first used as a name for the breed.
1877	The Clydesdale Horse Society forms in Scotland.
1879	The Clydesdale Breeders of the U.S.A. forms.
1970	Clydesdales are at risk of dying out.
2011	The number of Clydesdales around the world has reached about 5,000.

Glossary

ancestor: someone who lived before someone else in a family

breed: a group of animals that share features different from other groups of the kind. Also, to choose which animals should come together to make babies.

carriage: a wheeled cart carrying people and drawn by horses

cavalry: the part of the army made up of soldiers trained to fight on horseback

commercial: a way of selling goods or services on TV or radio

disabled: being unable to perform some of the tasks of daily life

draft: used to pull heavy loads

hand: a measurement used for a horse's height. One hand equals 4 inches (10.2 cm).

harness: a set of straps fixed together and fitted onto an animal so that it can be joined to a cart for pulling

mare: an adult female horse

muzzle: an animal's nose and mouth

stallion: an adult male horse

For More Information

Books

Dell, Pamela. *Clydesdales.* Chanhassen, MN: Child's World, 2007.

Diedrich, John. *The Clydesdale Horse.* Mankato, MN: Edge Books, 2005.

Rumsch, BreAnn. *Clydesdale Horses.* Edina, MN: ABDO Publishing, 2011.

Websites

Clydesdale Breeders of the U.S.A.
clydesusa.com
Learn about the history of Clydesdales and where you can find them today.

Clydesdales
www.seaworld.org/animal-info/info-books/clydesdale/index.htm
Read many facts about Clydesdales, including how they care for their young.